Homeowner Affordability and Stability Plan
Executive Summary

The deep contraction in the economy and in the housing market has created devastating consequences for homeowners and communities throughout the country.

- Millions of responsible families who make their monthly payments and fulfill their obligations have seen their property values fall, and are **now unable to refinance at lower mortgage rates.**

- Millions of workers have lost their jobs or had their hours cut back, are **now struggling to stay current on their mortgage payments** – with nearly 6 million households facing possible foreclosure.

- Neighborhoods are struggling, **as each foreclosed home reduces nearby property values** by as much as 9 percent.

The Homeowner Affordability and Stability Plan is part of the President's broad, comprehensive strategy to get the economy back on track. The plan will *help up to 7 to 9 million families restructure or refinance their mortgages to avoid foreclosure.* In doing so, the plan not only helps responsible homeowners on the verge of defaulting, but prevents neighborhoods and communities from being pulled over the edge too, as defaults and foreclosures contribute to falling home values, failing local businesses, and lost jobs. The key components of the Homeowner Affordability and Stability Plan are:

> *1. Refinancing for Up to 4 to 5 Million Responsible Homeowners to Make Their Mortgages More Affordable*
>
> *2. A $75 Billion Homeowner Stability Initiative to Reach Up to 3 to 4 Million At-Risk Homeowners*
>
> *3. Supporting Low Mortgage Rates By Strengthening Confidence in Fannie Mae and Freddie Mac*

1. **Affordability: Provide Access to Low-Cost Refinancing for Responsible Homeowners Suffering From Falling Home Prices**

   - *Enabling Up to 4 to 5 Million Responsible Homeowners to Refinance:* Mortgage rates are currently at historically low levels, providing homeowners with the opportunity to reduce their monthly payments by refinancing. But under current rules, most families who owe more than 80 percent of the value of their homes have a difficult time refinancing. Yet millions of responsible homeowners who put money down and made their mortgage payments on time have – through no fault of their own – seen the value of their homes drop low enough to make them unable to access these lower rates. As a result, the Obama Administration is announcing a new program that will help as many as 4 to 5 million responsible homeowners who took out conforming loans owned or guaranteed by Fannie Mae or Freddie Mac to refinance through those two institutions.

- *Reducing Monthly Payments:* For many families, a low-cost refinancing could reduce mortgage payments by thousands of dollars per year:

  o Consider a family that took out a 30-year fixed rate mortgage of $207,000 with an interest rate of 6.50% on a house worth $260,000 at the time. Today, that family has about $200,000 remaining on their mortgage, but the value of that home has fallen 15 percent to $221,000 – making them ineligible for today's low interest rates that now generally require the borrower to have 20 percent home equity. Under this refinancing plan, that family could refinance to a rate near 5.16% – reducing their annual payments by over $2,300.

2. **Stability: Create A $75 Billion Homeowner Stability Initiative to Reach Up to 3 to 4 Million At-Risk Homeowners**

- *Helping Hard-Pressed Homeowners Stay in their Homes:* This initiative is intended to reach millions of responsible homeowners who are struggling to afford their mortgage payments because of the current recession, yet cannot sell their homes because prices have fallen so significantly. Millions of hard-working families have seen their mortgage payments rise to 40 or even 50 percent of their monthly income – particularly those who received subprime and exotic loans with exploding terms and hidden fees. The Homeowner Stability Initiative helps those who commit to make reasonable monthly mortgage payments to stay in their homes – providing families with security and neighborhoods with stability.

- *No Aid for Speculators:* This initiative will go solely to helping homeowners who commit to make payments to stay in their home – it will not aid speculators or house flippers.

- *Protecting Neighborhoods:* This plan will also help to stabilize home prices for all homeowners in a neighborhood. When a home goes into foreclosure, the entire neighborhood is hurt. **The average homeowner could see his or her home value stabilized against declines in price by as much as $6,000** relative to what it would otherwise be absent the Homeowner Stability Initiative.

- *Providing Support for Responsible Homeowners:* Because loan modifications are more likely to succeed if they are made before a borrower misses a payment, the plan will include households at risk of imminent default despite being current on their mortgage payments.

- *Providing Loan Modifications to Bring Monthly Payments to Sustainable Levels:* The Homeowner Stability Initiative has a simple goal: reduce the amount homeowners owe per month to sustainable levels. Using money allocated under the Financial Stability Plan and the full strength of Fannie Mae and Freddie Mac, this program has several key components:

  - *A Shared Effort to Reduce Monthly Payments:* For a sample household with payments adding up to 43 percent of his monthly income, the lender would first be responsible for bringing down interest rates so that the borrower's monthly mortgage payment is no more than 38 percent of his or her income. Next, the initiative would match further reductions in interest payments dollar-for-dollar with the lender to bring that ratio down to 31 percent. If that borrower had a $220,000 mortgage, that could mean a reduction in monthly payments by over $400. That lower interest rate must be kept in place for five years, after which it

2

could gradually be stepped up to the conforming loan rate in place at the time of the modification. Lenders will also be able to bring down monthly payments by reducing the principal owed on the mortgage, with Treasury sharing in the costs.

- *"Pay for Success" Incentives to Servicers:* Servicers will receive an up-front fee of $1,000 for each eligible modification meeting guidelines established under this initiative. They will also receive "pay for success" fees – awarded monthly as long as the borrower stays current on the loan – of up to $1,000 each year for three years.

- *Incentives to Help Borrowers Stay Current:* To provide an extra incentive for borrowers to keep paying on time, the initiative will provide a monthly balance reduction payment that goes straight towards reducing the principal balance of the mortgage loan. As long as a borrower stays current on his or her loan, he or she can get up to $1,000 each year for five years.

- *Reaching Borrowers Early:* To keep lenders focused on reaching borrowers who are trying their best to stay current on their mortgages, an incentive payment of $500 will be paid to servicers, and an incentive payment of $1,500 will be paid to mortgage holders, if they modify at-risk loans before the borrower falls behind.

- *Home Price Decline Reserve Payments:* To encourage lenders to modify more mortgages and enable more families to keep their homes, the Administration -- together with the FDIC -- has developed an innovative partial guarantee initiative. The insurance fund – to be created by the Treasury Department at a size of up to $10 billion – will be designed to discourage lenders from opting to foreclose on mortgages that could be viable now out of fear that home prices will fall even further later on. Holders of mortgages modified under the program would be provided with an additional insurance payment on each modified loan, linked to declines in the home price index.

- ***Institute Clear and Consistent Guidelines for Loan Modifications:*** Treasury will develop uniform guidance for loan modifications across the mortgage industry, working closely with the bank agencies and building on the FDIC's pioneering work. The Guidelines will be used for the Administration's new foreclosure prevention plan. Moreover, all financial institutions receiving Financial Stability Plan financial assistance going forward will be required to implement loan modification plans consistent with Treasury Guidance. Fannie Mae and Freddie Mac will use these guidelines for loans that they own or guarantee, and the Administration will work with regulators and other federal and state agencies to implement these guidelines across the entire mortgage market. The agencies will seek to apply these guidelines when permissible and appropriate to all loans owned or guaranteed by the federal government, including those owned or guaranteed by Ginnie Mae, the Federal Housing Administration, Treasury, the Federal Reserve, the FDIC, Veterans' Affairs and the Department of Agriculture.

- *Other Comprehensive Measures to Reduce Foreclosure and Strengthen Communities*

  - *Require Strong Oversight, Reporting and Quarterly Meetings with Treasury, the FDIC, the Federal Reserve and HUD to Monitor Performance*

  - *Allow Judicial Modifications of Home Mortgages During Bankruptcy for Borrowers Who Have Run Out of Options*

  - *Provide $1.5 Billion in Relocation and Other Forms of Assistance to Renters Displaced by Foreclosure and $2 Billion in Neighborhood Stabilization Funds*

  - *Improve the Flexibility of Hope for Homeowners and Other FHA Programs to Modify and Refinance At-Risk Borrowers*

3. **Supporting Low Mortgage Rates By Strengthening Confidence in Fannie Mae and Freddie Mac:**

   - ***Ensuring Strength and Security of the Mortgage Market:*** Today, using funds already authorized in 2008 by Congress for this purpose, the Treasury Department is increasing its funding commitment to Fannie Mae and Freddie Mac to ensure the strength and security of the mortgage market and to help maintain mortgage affordability.

     - ***Provide Forward-Looking Confidence:*** The increased funding will enable Fannie Mae and Freddie Mac to carry out ambitious efforts to ensure mortgage affordability for responsible homeowners, and provide forward-looking confidence in the mortgage market.

     - Treasury is increasing its Preferred Stock Purchase Agreements to $200 billion each from their original level of $100 billion each.

   - ***Promoting Stability and Liquidity:*** In addition, the Treasury Department will continue to purchase Fannie Mae and Freddie Mac mortgage-backed securities to promote stability and liquidity in the marketplace.

   - ***Increasing The Size of Mortgage Portfolios:*** To ensure that Fannie Mae and Freddie Mac can continue to provide assistance in addressing problems in the housing market, Treasury will also be increasing the size of the GSEs' retained mortgage portfolios allowed under the agreements – by $50 billion to $900 billion – along with corresponding increases in the allowable debt outstanding.

   - ***Support State Housing Finance Agencies:*** The Administration will work with Fannie Mae and Freddie Mac to support state housing finance agencies in serving homebuyers.

   - ***No EESA or Financial Stability Plan Money:*** The $200 billion in funding commitments are being made under the Housing and Economic Recovery Act and **do not use any money from the Financial Stability Plan or Emergency Economic Stabilization Act/TARP.**

Homeowner Affordability and Stability Plan
Fact Sheet

The deep contraction in the economy and in the housing market has created devastating consequences for homeowners and communities throughout the country. Millions of responsible families who make their monthly payments and fulfill their obligations have seen their property values fall, and are now unable to refinance to lower mortgage rates. Meanwhile, millions of workers have lost their jobs or had their hours cut, and are now struggling to stay current on their mortgage payments. As a result, as many as 6 million families are expected to face foreclosure in the next several years, with millions more struggling to stay current on their payments.

The present crisis is real, but temporary. As home prices fall, demand for housing will increase, and conditions will ultimately find a new balance. Yet in the absence of decisive action, we risk an intensifying spiral in which lenders foreclose, pushing home prices still lower, reducing the value of household savings, and making it harder for all families to refinance. In some studies, foreclosure on a home has been found to reduce the prices of nearby homes by as much as 9 percent — creating the potential that even borrowers who make every payment suffer from an increase in foreclosures in their community.

The Obama Administration's Homeowner Affordability and Stability Plan *will offer assistance to as many as 7 to 9 million homeowners* making a good-faith effort to stay current on their mortgage payments, while attempting to prevent the destructive impact of foreclosures on families and communities. It will not provide money to speculators, and it will target support to the working homeowners who have made every possible effort to stay current on their mortgage payments. Just as the American Recovery and Reinvestment Act works to save or create several million new jobs and the Financial Stability Plan works to get credit flowing, the Homeowner Affordability and Stability Plan will support a recovery in the housing market and ensure that these workers can continue paying off their mortgages.

By supporting low mortgage rates by strengthening confidence in Fannie Mae and Freddie Mac, providing up to 4 to 5 million homeowners with new access to refinancing and enacting a comprehensive stability initiative to offer reduced monthly payments for up to 3 to 4 million at-risk homeowners, this plan – which draws off the best ideas developed within the Administration, as well as from Congressional housing leaders and Federal Deposit Insurance Corporation Chair Sheila Bair – brings together the government, lenders and borrowers to share responsibility towards ensuring working Americans can afford to stay in their homes.

Homeowner Affordability and Stability Plan

1. **Refinancing for Responsible Homeowners Suffering From Falling Home Prices**

2. **A Comprehensive $75 Billion Homeowner Stability Initiative**

   - A Loan Modification Plan To Reach 3 to 4 Million Homeowners
     - Shared Effort with Lenders to Reduce Interest Payments
     - Incentives to Servicers and Borrowers
   - Clear and Consistent Guidelines for Loan Modifications
   - Required Participation By Financial Stability Plan Participants
   - Modifications of Home Mortgages During Bankruptcy
   - Strengthen Hope for Homeowners and Other FHA Loan Programs
   - Support Local Communities and Help Displaced Renters

3. **Support Low Mortgage Rates by Strengthening Confidence in Fannie Mae and Freddie Mac**

---

1. **Provide Access to Low-Cost Refinancing for Responsible Homeowners Suffering From Falling Home Prices:**

   - *Provide the Opportunity for Up to 4 to 5 Million Responsible Homeowners Expected to Refinance:* Mortgage rates are currently at historically low levels, providing homeowners with the opportunity to reduce their monthly payments by refinancing. But under current rules, most families who owe more than 80 percent of the value of their homes have a difficult time securing refinancing. (For example, if a borrower's home was worth $200,000, he or she would have limited refinancing options if he or she owed more than $160,000.) Yet millions of responsible homeowners who put money down and made their mortgage payments on time have – through no fault of their own – seen the value of their homes drop low enough to make them unable to access these lower rates. As a result, the Obama Administration is announcing <u>a new program that will provide the opportunity for 4 to 5 million responsible homeowners who took out conforming loans owned or guaranteed by Freddie Mac and Fannie Mae to refinance through the two institutions over time.</u>

   - *Reducing Monthly Payments:* For many families, a low-cost refinancing could reduce mortgage payments by thousands of dollars per year. For example, consider a family that took a 30-year fixed rate mortgage of $207,000 with an interest rate of 6.50% on a house worth $260,000 at the time. Today, that family has $200,000 remaining on their mortgage, but the value of that home has fallen 15 percent to $221,000 – making them ineligible for today's low interest rates that generally require the borrower to have 20 percent home equity. Under this refinancing plan, that family could refinance to a rate near 5.16% – reducing their annual payments by over $2,300.

2. **A $75 Billion Homeowner Stability Initiative to Prevent Foreclosures and Help Responsible Families Stay in Their Homes:** The Treasury Department, working with the GSEs, FHA, the FDIC and other federal agencies, will undertake a comprehensive multi-part strategy to prevent millions of foreclosures and help families stay in their homes. This strategy includes the following five features:

   - *A Homeowner Stability Initiative to Reach Up to 3 to 4 Million At-Risk Homeowners*

   - *Clear and Consistent Guidelines for Loan Modifications*

   - *Requiring That Financial Stability Plan Recipients Use Guidance for Loan Modifications*

   - *Allowing Judicial Modifications of Home Mortgages During Bankruptcy When A Borrower Has No Other Options*

   - *Require Strong Oversight, Reporting and Quarterly Meetings with Treasury, the FDIC, the Federal Reserve and HUD to Monitor Performance*

   - *Strengthening FHA Programs and Providing Support for Local Communities*

A. ***A Homeowner Stability Initiative to Reach Up to 3 to 4 Million At-Risk Homeowners:***
This initiative is intended to reach millions of responsible homeowners who are
struggling to afford their mortgage payments because of the current recession, yet cannot
sell their homes because prices have fallen so significantly. In the current economy, in
which 3.6 million jobs have been lost over the past 14 months, millions of hard-working
families have seen their mortgage payments rise to 40 or even 50 percent of their monthly
income – particularly if they received subprime and exotic loans with exploding terms
and hidden fees. The Homeowner Stability Initiative operates through a shared
partnership to temporarily help those who commit to make reasonable monthly mortgage
payments to stay in their homes, providing families with security and neighborhoods with
stability. This plan will also help to stabilize home prices for homeowners in
neighborhoods hardest hit by foreclosures. Based on estimates concerning the
relationship between foreclosures and home prices, with the average house in the U.S.
valued around $200,000, **the average homeowner could see his or her home value
stabilized against declines in price by as much as $6,000** relative to what it would
otherwise be absent the Homeowner Stability Initiative.

Who the Program Reaches:

- ***Focusing on Homeowners At Risk:*** Anyone with <u>high combined mortgage debt
compared to income</u> or who <u>is "underwater"</u> (with a combined mortgage balance
higher than the current market value of his house) may be eligible for a loan
modification. This initiative will also include borrowers who show other indications
of being at risk of default. Eligibility for the program will sunset at the end of three
years.

- ***Reaching Homeowners Who Have Not Missed Payments:*** Delinquency will not be a
requirement for eligibility. Rather, because loan modifications are more likely to
succeed if they are made before a borrower misses a payment, the plan will include
households at risk of imminent default despite being current on their mortgage
payments.

- ***Common Sense Restrictions:*** Only owner-occupied homes qualify; no home
mortgages larger than the Freddie/Fannie conforming limits will be eligible. *This
initiative will go solely to supporting responsible homeowners willing to make
payments to stay in their home – it will not aid speculators or house flippers.*

- ***Special Provisions for Families with High Total Debt Levels:*** Borrowers with high
total debt qualify, but only if they agree to enter HUD-certified consumer debt
counseling. Specifically, homeowners with total "back end" debt (which includes not
only housing debt, but other debt including car loans and credit card debt) equal to
55% or more of their income will be required to agree to enter a counseling program
as a condition for a modification.

How the Program Works

- The Homeowner Stability Initiative has a simple goal: reduce the amount
homeowners owe per month to sustainable levels. This program will bring together
lenders, servicers, borrowers, and the government, so that **all stakeholders share in**

the cost of ensuring that responsible homeowners can afford their monthly mortgage payments – helping to reach up to 3 to 4 million at-risk borrowers in all segments of the mortgage market, reducing foreclosures, and helping to avoid further downward pressures on overall home prices. The program has several key components:

i. ***Shared Effort to Reduce Monthly Payments:*** Treasury will partner with financial institutions to reduce homeowners' monthly mortgage payments.

- The lender will have to <u>first reduce interest rates on mortgages to a specified affordability level</u> (specifically, bring down rates so that the borrower's monthly mortgage payment is no greater than 38% of his or her income).

- Next, <u>the initiative will match further reductions in interest payments dollar-for-dollar</u> with the lender, down to a 31% debt-to-income ratio for the borrower.

- To ensure long-term affordability, <u>lenders will keep the modified payments in place for five years</u>. After that point, the interest rate can be gradually stepped-up to the conforming loan rate in place at the time of the modification. *Note: Lenders can also bring down monthly payments to these affordability targets through reducing the amount of mortgage principal. The initiative will provide a partial share of the costs of this principal reduction, up to the amount the lender would have received for an interest rate reduction.*

ii. ***"Pay f or Success" Incentives to Servicers:*** Servicers will receive an up-front fee of $1,000 for each eligible modification meeting guidelines established under this initiative. Servicers will also receive "pay for success" fees – awarded monthly as long as the borrower stays current on the loan – of up to $1,000 each year for three years.

iii. ***Responsible Modification Incentives:*** Because loan modifications are more likely to succeed if they are made before a borrower misses a payment, the plan will include an incentive payment of $1,500 to mortgage holders and $500 for servicers for modifications made while a borrower at risk of imminent default is still current.

iv. ***Incentives to Help Borrowers Stay Current:*** To provide an extra incentive for borrowers to keep paying on time under the modified loan, the initiative will <u>provide a monthly balance reduction payment that goes straight towards reducing the principal balance on the mortgage loan.</u> As long as the borrower stays current on his or her payments, he or she can get up to $1,000 each year for five years.

v. ***Home Price Decline Reserve Payments:*** To encourage lenders to modify more mortgages and enable more families to keep their homes, the Administration -- together with the FDIC -- has developed an innovative partial guarantee initiative. The insurance fund – to be created by the Treasury Department at a size of up to $10 billion – will be designed to discourage lenders from opting to foreclose on mortgages that could be viable now out of fear that home prices will fall even further later on. This initiative provides lenders with the security to undertake more mortgage modifications by assuring that if home price declines are worse than expected, they have reserves to fall back on. Holders of mortgages modified under the program would be provided with an additional insurance payment on each modified loan, linked to declines in the home price index. These payments could be set aside as reserves, providing a partial guarantee in the event that home price declines – and therefore losses in cases of default – are higher than expected.

How It Will Be Effective

- **Protecting Taxpayers:** To protect taxpayers, the Homeowner Stability Initiative will focus on sound modifications. If the total expected cost of a modification for a lender taking into account the government payments is expected to be higher than the direct costs of putting the homeowner through foreclosure, that borrower will not be eligible. For those borrowers unable to maintain homeownership, even under the affordable terms offered, the plan will provide incentives to encourage families and lenders to avoid the costly foreclosure process and minimize the damage that foreclosure imposes on lenders, borrowers and communities alike. Moreover, Treasury will not provide subsidies to reduce interest rates on modified loans to levels below 2%.

- **Counseling and Outreach to Maximize Participation:** Under the plan, the Department of Housing and Urban Development will also make available funding for non-profit counseling agencies to improve outreach and communications, especially to disadvantaged communities and those hardest-hit by foreclosures and vacancies.

- **Creating Proper Oversight and Tracking Data to Ensure Program Success:** Fannie Mae and Freddie Mac will be responsible – subject to Treasury's oversight and the Federal Housing Finance Agency's conservatorship – for monitoring compliance by servicers with the program. Every servicer participating in the program will be required to report standardized loan-level data on modifications, borrower and property characteristics, and outcomes. The data will be pooled so the government and private sector can measure success and make changes where needed. Treasury will meet quarterly with the FDIC, the Federal Reserve, the Department of Housing and Urban Development and the Federal Housing Finance Agency to ensure that the program is on track to meeting its goals.

- **Limiting the Impact of Foreclosure When Modification Doesn't Work:** Lenders will receive incentives to take alternatives to foreclosures, like short sales or taking of deeds in lieu of foreclosure. Treasury will also work with the GSEs to provide data on foreclosed properties to streamline the process of selling or redeveloping them, thereby ensuring that they do not remain vacant and unsold.

B. **Clear and Consistent Guidelines for Loan Modifications:** A lack of common standards has limited loan modifications, even when they are likely to both reduce the chance of foreclosure and raise the value of the securities owned by investors. Mortgage servicers – who should have an interest in instituting common-sense loan modifications – often refrain from doing so because they fear lawsuits. Clear and consistent guidelines for modifications are a key component of foreclosure prevention.

- ***Developing Clear and Consistent Guidelines for Loan Modifications:*** Working with the FDIC, other federal banking and credit union regulators, the FHA and the Federal Housing Finance Agency, the Administration is in process of developing guidelines for sustainable mortgage modifications for all federal agencies and the private sector – <u>bringing order and consistency to foreclosure mitigation.</u> The guidelines will include detailed protocols for loss mitigation as well for identifying borrowers at risk of default; the Administration expects to announce these guidelines by Wednesday, March 4th

- ***Applying Guidelines Across Government and the Private Sector:*** Treasury will develop uniform guidance for loan modifications across the mortgage industry by working closely with the FDIC and other bank agencies and building on the FDIC's pioneering role in developing a systematic loan modification process last year. The Guidelines – to be posted online – will be used for the Administration's new foreclosure prevention plan. Moreover, all financial institutions receiving Financial Stability Plan financial assistance going forward will be required to implement loan modification plans consistent with Treasury guidance. Fannie Mae and Freddie Mac will use these guidelines for loans that they own or guarantee, and the Administration will work with regulators and other federal and state agencies to implement these guidelines across the entire mortgage market. The agencies will seek to apply these guidelines when permissible and appropriate to all loans owned or guaranteed by the federal government, including those owned or guaranteed by Ginnie Mae, the Federal Housing Administration, Treasury, the Federal Reserve, the FDIC, Veterans' Affairs and the Department of Agriculture. In addition, these guidelines will apply to loans owned or serviced by insured financial institutions supervised by the Office of the Comptroller of the Currency, the Office of Thrift Supervision, the Federal Reserve, the Federal Deposit Insurance Corporation and the National Credit Union Administration.

C. ***<u>Requiring All Financial Stability Plan Recipients to Use Guidance for Loan Modifications:</u>*** As announced last week, the Treasury Department will <u>require all Financial Stability Plan recipients going forward to participate in foreclosure mitigation plans</u> consistent with Treasury's loan modification guidelines.

D. ***<u>Allowing Judicial Modifications of Home Mortgages During Bankruptcy for Borrowers Who Have Run Out of Options:</u>*** The Obama administration will seek careful changes to personal bankruptcy provisions so that bankruptcy judges can modify mortgages written in the past few years when families run out of other options.

- ***How Judicial Modification Works:*** When an individual enters personal bankruptcy proceedings, his mortgage loans in excess of the current value of his property will now be treated as unsecured. This will allow a bankruptcy judge to <u>develop an affordable plan for the homeowner to continue making payments</u>. To receive judicial modifications in bankruptcy, homeowners must first ask their servicers/lenders for a modification and certify that they have complied with reasonable requests from the servicer to provide essential information. *This provision will apply only to existing mortgages under Fannie Mae and Freddie Mac conforming loan limits, so that millionaire homes don't clog the bankruptcy courts.*

6

- *Bolster FHA and VA Authority to Protect Investors and Ensure Loan Modifications Occur:* Legislation will provide the FHA and VA with the authority they need to provide partial claims in the event of bankruptcy or voluntary modification so that holders of loans guaranteed by the FHA and VA are not disadvantaged.

E. *Strengthening FHA Programs and Providing Support for Local Communities*

- *Ease Restrictions in Federal Housing Administration Programs, Including Hope for Homeowners:* The Hope for Homeowners program offers one avenue for struggling borrowers to refinance their mortgages. In order to ensure that more homeowners participate, the FHA will reduce fees paid by borrowers, increase flexibility for lenders to modify troubled loans, permit borrowers with higher debt loads to qualify, and allow payments to servicers of the existing loans.

- *Strengthening Communities Hardest Hit by the Financial and Housing Crises:* As part of the recovery plan signed by the President, the Department of Housing and Urban Development will award $2 billion in competitive Neighborhood Stabilization Program grants for innovative programs that reduce foreclosure. Additionally, the recovery plan includes an additional $1.5 billion to provide renter assistance, reducing homelessness and avoiding entry into shelters

3. **Support Low Mortgage Rates By Strengthening Confidence in Fannie Mae and Freddie Mac:**

- *Ensuring Strength and Security of the Mortgage Market:* Today, using funds already authorized in 2008 by Congress for this purpose, the Treasury Department is increasing its funding commitment to Fannie Mae and Freddie Mac to ensure the strength and security of the mortgage market and to help maintain mortgage affordability.

  o *Provide Forward-Looking Confidence:* The increased funding will enable Fannie Mae and Freddie Mac to carry out ambitious efforts to ensure mortgage affordability for responsible homeowners, and provide forward-looking confidence in the mortgage market.

  o Treasury is increasing its Preferred Stock Purchase Agreements to $200 billion each from their original level of $100 billion each.

- *Promoting Stability and Liquidity:* In addition, the Treasury Department will continue to purchase Fannie Mae and Freddie Mac mortgage-backed securities to promote stability and liquidity in the marketplace.

- *Increasing The Size of Mortgage Portfolios:* To ensure that Fannie Mae and Freddie Mac can continue to provide assistance in addressing problems in the housing market, Treasury will also be increasing the size of the GSEs' retained mortgage portfolios allowed under the agreements – by $50 billion to $900 billion – along with corresponding increases in the allowable debt outstanding.

- ***Support State Housing Finance Agencies:*** The Administration will work with Fannie Mae and Freddie Mac to support state housing finance agencies in serving homebuyers.

- ***No EESA or Financial Stability Plan Money:*** The $200 billion in funding commitments are being made under the Housing and Economic Recovery Act and **do not use any money from the Financial Stability Plan or Emergency Economic Stabilization Act/TARP.**

Questions and Answers for Borrowers about the

Homeowner Affordability and Stability Plan

Borrowers Who Are Current on Their Mortgage Are Asking:

1. **What help is available for borrowers who stay current on their mortgage payments but have seen their homes decrease in value?**

   Under the Homeowner Affordability and Stability Plan, eligible borrowers who stay current on their mortgages but have been unable to refinance to lower their interest rates because their homes have decreased in value, may now have the opportunity to refinance into a 30 or 15 year, fixed rate loan. Through the program, Fannie Mae and Freddie Mac will allow the refinancing of mortgage loans that they hold in their portfolios or that they placed in mortgage backed securities.

2. **I owe more than my property is worth, do I still qualify to refinance under the Homeowner Affordability and Stability Plan?**

   Eligible loans will now include those where the new first mortgage (including any refinancing costs) will not exceed 105% of the current market value of the property. For example, if your property is worth $200,000 but you owe $210,000 or less you may qualify. The current value of your property will be determined after you apply to refinance.

3. **How do I know if I am eligible?**

   Complete eligibility details will be announced on March 4th when the program starts. The criteria for eligibility will include having sufficient income to make the new payment and an acceptable mortgage payment history. The program is limited to loans held or securitized by Fannie Mae or Freddie Mac.

4. **I have both a first and a second mortgage. Do I still qualify to refinance under the Homeowner Affordability and Stability Plan?**

   As long as the amount due on the first mortgage is less than 105% of the value of the property, borrowers with more than one mortgage may be eligible to refinance under the Homeowner Affordability and Stability Plan. Your eligibility will depend, in part, on agreement by the lender that has your second mortgage to remain in a second position, and on your ability to meet the new payment terms on the first mortgage.

5. **Will refinancing lower my payments?**

   The objective of the Homeowner Affordability and Stability Plan is to provide creditworthy borrowers who have shown a commitment to paying their mortgage with affordable payments that are sustainable for the life of the loan. Borrowers whose mortgage interest rates are much higher than the current market rate should see an immediate reduction in their payments. Borrowers who are paying interest only, or who have a low introductory rate that will increase in the future, may not see their current payment go down if they refinance to a fixed rate. These borrowers, however, could save a great deal over the life of the loan. When you submit a loan application, your lender will give you a "Good Faith Estimate" that includes your new interest rate, mortgage payment and the amount that you will pay over the life of the loan. Compare this to your current loan terms. If it is not an improvement, a refinancing may not be right for you.

6. **What are the interest rate and other terms of this refinance offer?**

The objective of the Homeowner Affordability and Stability Plan is to provide borrowers with a safe loan program with a fixed, affordable payment. All loans refinanced under the plan will have a 30 or 15 year term with a fixed interest rate. The rate will be based on market rates in effect at the time of the refinance and any associated points and fees quoted by the lender. Interest rates may vary across lenders and over time as market rates adjust. The refinanced loans will have no prepayment penalties or balloon notes.

7. **Will refinancing reduce the amount that I owe on my loan?**

No. The objective of the Homeowner Affordability and Stability Plan is to help borrowers refinance into safer, more affordable fixed rate loans. Refinancing will not reduce the amount you owe to the first mortgage holder or any other debt you owe. However, by reducing the interest rate, refinancing should save you money by reducing the amount of interest that you repay over the life of the loan.

8. **How do I know if my loan is owned or has been securitized by Fannie Mae or Freddie Mac?**

To determine if your loan is owned or has been securitized by Fannie Mae or Freddie Mac and is eligible to be refinanced, you should contact your mortgage lender after March 4, 2009.

9. **When can I apply?**

Mortgage lenders will begin accepting applications after the details of the program are announced on March 4, 2009.

10. **What should I do in the meantime?**

You should gather the information that you will need to provide to your lender after March 4, when the refinance program becomes available. This includes:

- information about the gross monthly income of all borrowers, including your most recent pay stubs if you receive them or documentation of income you receive from other sources

- your most recent income tax return

- information about any second mortgage on the house

- payments on each of your credit cards if you are carrying balances from month to month, and

- payments on other loans such as student loans and car loans.

Borrowers Who Are at Risk of Foreclosure Are Asking:

1. **What help is available for borrowers who are at risk of foreclosure either because they are behind on their mortgage or are struggling to make the payments?**

    The Homeowner Affordability and Stability Plan offers help to borrowers who are already behind on their mortgage payments or who are struggling to keep their loans current. By providing mortgage lenders with financial incentives to modify existing first mortgages, the Treasury hopes to help as many as 3 to 4 million homeowners avoid foreclosure regardless of who owns or services the mortgage.

2. **Do I need to be behind on my mortgage payments to be eligible for a modification?**

    No. Borrowers who are struggling to stay current on their mortgage payments may be eligible if their income is not sufficient to continue to make their mortgage payments and they are at risk of imminent default. This may be due to several factors, such as a loss of income, a significant increase in expenses, or an interest rate that will reset to an unaffordable level.

3. **How do I know if I qualify for a payment reduction under the Homeowner Affordability and Stability Plan?**

    In general, you may qualify for a mortgage modification if (a) you occupy your house as your primary residence; (b) your monthly mortgage payment is greater than 31% of your monthly gross income; and (c) your loan is not large enough to exceed current Fannie Mae and Freddie Mac loan limits. Final eligibility will be determined by your mortgage lender based on your financial situation and detailed guidelines that will be available on March 4, 2009.

4. **I do not live in the house that secures the mortgage I'd like to modify. Is this mortgage eligible for the Homeowner Affordability and Stability Plan?**

No. For example, if you own a house that you use as a vacation home or that you rent out to tenants, the mortgage on that house is not eligible. If you used to live in the home but you moved out, the mortgage is not eligible. Only the mortgage on your primary residence is eligible. The mortgage lender will check to see if the dwelling is your primary residence.

5. **I have a mortgage on a duplex. I live in one unit and rent the other. Will I still be eligible?**

Yes. Mortgages on 2, 3 and 4 unit properties are eligible as long as you live in one unit as your primary residence.

6. **I have two mortgages. Will the Homeowner Affordability and Stability Plan reduce the payments on both?**

Only the first mortgage is eligible for a modification.

7. **I owe more than my house is worth. Will the Homeowner Affordability and Stability Plan reduce what I owe?**

The primary objective of the Homeowner Affordability and Stability Plan is to help borrowers avoid foreclosure by modifying troubled loans to achieve a payment the borrower can afford. Lenders are likely to lower payments mainly by reducing loan interest rates. However, the program offers incentives for principal reductions and at your lender's discretion modifications may include upfront reductions of loan principal.

8. **I heard the government was providing a financial incentive to borrowers. Is that true?**

Yes. To encourage borrowers who work hard to retain homeownership, the Homeowner Affordability and Stability Plan provides incentive payments as a borrower makes timely payments on the modified loan. The incentive will accrue on a monthly basis and will be applied directly to reduce your mortgage debt. Borrowers who pay on time for five years can have up to $5,000 applied to reduce their debt by the end of that period.

9. **How much will a modification cost me?**

There is no cost to borrowers for a modification under the Homeowner Affordability and Stability Plan. If you wish to get assistance from a HUD-approved housing counseling agency or are referred to a counselor as a condition of the modification, you will not be charged a fee. Borrowers should beware of any organization that attempts to charge a fee for housing counseling or modification of a delinquent loan, especially if they require a fee in advance.

10. **Is my lender required to modify my loan?**

No. Mortgage lenders participate in the program on a voluntary basis and loans are evaluated for modification on a case-by-case basis. But the government is offering substantial incentives and it is expected that most major lenders will participate.

11. **I'm already working with my lender / housing counselor on a loan workout. Can I still be considered for the Homeowner Affordability and Stability Plan?**

Ask your lender or counselor to be considered under the Homeowner Affordability and Stability Plan.

12. **How do I apply for a modification under the Homeowner Affordability and Stability Plan?**

You may not need to do anything at this time. Most mortgage lenders will evaluate loans in their portfolio to identify borrowers who may meet the eligibility criteria. After March 4 they will send letters to potentially eligible homeowners, a process that may take several weeks. If you think you qualify for a modification and do not receive a letter within several weeks, contact your mortgage servicer or a HUD-approved housing counselor. Please be aware that servicers and counseling agencies are expected to receive an extraordinary number of calls about this program.

13. **What should I do in the meantime?**

You should gather the information that you will need to provide to your lender on or after March 4, when the modification program becomes available. This includes

- information about the monthly gross income of your household including recent pay stubs if you receive them or documentation of income you receive from other sources

- your most recent income tax return

- information about any second mortgage on the house

- payments on each of your credit cards if you are carrying balances from month to month, and

- payments on other loans such as student loans and car loans.

14. **My loan is scheduled for foreclosure soon. What should I do?**

Contact your mortgage servicer or credit counselor. Many mortgage lenders have expressed their intention to postpone foreclosure sales on all mortgages that may qualify for the modification in order to allow sufficient time to evaluate the borrower's eligibility. We support this effort.

Preserving Homeownership: Foreclosure Prevention Initiatives

Katie Jones
Analyst in Housing Policy

February 25, 2009

Congressional Research Service

7-5700
www.crs.gov
R40210

CRS Report for Congress —————————————————————
Prepared for Members and Committees of Congress

Summary

The foreclosure rate in the United States has been rising rapidly since the middle of 2006. Losing a home to foreclosure can hurt homeowners in many ways; for example, homeowners who have been through a foreclosure may have difficulty finding a new place to live or obtaining a loan in the future. Furthermore, concentrated foreclosures can drag down nearby home prices, and large numbers of abandoned properties can negatively affect communities. Finally, the increase in foreclosures may destabilize the housing market, which could in turn negatively impact the economy as a whole.

Because of the many negative consequences associated with rising foreclosure rates, there is a broad consensus that the government should explore efforts to prevent further increases in foreclosures and help more families preserve homeownership. Several federal, state, and local foreclosure prevention initiatives have been launched to date. These programs include the expired *FHASecure* program and the Hope for Homeowners program, both of which allowed troubled borrowers to refinance their loans into new mortgages backed by the Federal Housing Administration (FHA); a loan modification program set up by Fannie Mae and Freddie Mac for mortgages held by those institutions; and a program put in place by the Federal Deposit Insurance Corporation (FDIC) to help troubled borrowers with loans that had been owned by IndyMac Bank before it was taken over by the FDIC. Several states and localities have initiated their own foreclosure prevention efforts, as have private companies including Bank of America, JP Morgan Chase, and Citigroup. A voluntary alliance of mortgage lenders, servicers, investors, and housing counselors has also formed the HOPE NOW Alliance to reach out to troubled borrowers.

On February 18, 2009, President Obama announced the Homeowner Affordability and Stability plan, which aims to modify the loans of borrowers who are in danger of default or foreclosure. On February 23, 2009, Representative John Conyers introduced H.R. 1106, the Helping Families Save Their Homes Act of 2009. This bill would make changes to the Hope for Homeowners program, amend bankruptcy law to allow judges to modify mortgages on primary residences, and establish a safe harbor for servicers who engage in certain loan modifications.

While many observers agree that more needs to be done to prevent foreclosures, there are several challenges associated with foreclosure mitigation plans. These challenges include implementation issues, such as deciding who has the authority to make mortgage modifications, developing the capacity to complete widespread modifications, and assessing the possibility that homeowners with modified loans will nevertheless default again in the future. Other challenges are related to the perception of fairness, the problem of inadvertently providing incentives for borrowers to default, and the possibility of setting an unwanted precedent for future mortgage lending.

This report describes the consequences of foreclosure on homeowners, outlines recent foreclosure prevention plans implemented by the government and private organizations, and discusses the challenges associated with foreclosure prevention. It will be updated as events warrant.

Contents

Introduction and Background 1
    Recent Market Trends 1
    Impacts of Foreclosure 3
    The Policy Problem 3
    Why Might a Household Find Itself Facing Foreclosure? 4
        Changes in Household Circumstances 4
        Mortgage Features 5
    Types of Loan Workouts 7
        Repayment Plans 8
        Principal Forbearance 8
        Principal Write-Downs/Principal Forgiveness 8
        Interest Rate Reductions 8
        Extended Loan Term/Extended Amortization 9
Recent Foreclosure Prevention Initiatives 9
    Government Initiatives 9
        FHASecure 9
        IndyMac Loan Modifications 11
        Hope for Homeowners 12
        Fannie Mae and Freddie Mac 13
        Federal Reserve 14
        The Homeowner Affordability and Stability Plan 14
        Foreclosure Counseling Funding to NeighborWorks America 15
        State and Local Initiatives 16
    Private Initiatives 16
        HOPE NOW Alliance 16
        Bank of America 17
        JP Morgan Chase 18
        Citigroup 18
Other Foreclosure Prevention Proposals 19
    Changing Bankruptcy Law 19
    Foreclosure Moratorium 19
    Federal Deposit Insurance Corporation Plan 20
    Use of TARP Funds 20
Issues and Challenges Associated with Preventing Foreclosures 20
    Who Has The Authority to Modify Mortgages? 20
    Volume of Delinquencies and Foreclosures 21
    Possibility of Re-Default 21
    Fairness Issues 22
    Incentives 22
    Precedent 22

Figures

Figure 1. Percentage of Loans in Foreclosure by Type of Loan 2

Tables

Table A-1. Features of Selected Programs 24

Appendixes

Appendix. Comparison of Recent Federal Foreclosure Prevention Initiatives 24

Contacts

Author Contact Information 26

Introduction and Background

The foreclosure rate in the United States has been rising rapidly since around the middle of 2006. The large increase in home foreclosures since that time has negatively impacted individual households, local communities, and the economy as a whole. Consequently, an issue before Congress is whether to use federal resources and authority to help prevent further increases in home foreclosures and, if so, how to best accomplish this objective. This report details the impact of foreclosure on homeowners. It also describes recent attempts to preserve homeownership that have been implemented by the government and private lenders, and briefly outlines current proposals for further foreclosure prevention activities. It concludes with a discussion of some of the challenges inherent in designing foreclosure prevention initiatives. This report will be updated as events warrant.

Foreclosure refers to formal legal proceedings initiated by a mortgage lender against a homeowner after the homeowner has missed a certain number of payments on his or her mortgage.[1] When a foreclosure is completed, the homeowner loses his or her home, which is either repossessed by the lender or sold at auction to repay the outstanding debt. In general, the term "foreclosure" can refer to the foreclosure process or the completion of a foreclosure. This report deals primarily with preventing foreclosure completions.

In order for the foreclosure process to begin, two things must happen: a homeowner must fail to make a certain number of payments on his or her mortgage, and a lender must decide to initiate foreclosure proceedings rather than pursue other options (such as offering a repayment plan or a loan modification). A borrower that misses one or more payments is usually referred to as being delinquent on a loan; when a borrower has missed three or more payments, he or she is generally considered to be in default. Lenders can choose to begin foreclosure proceedings after a homeowner defaults on his or her mortgage, although lenders vary in how quickly they begin foreclosure proceedings after a borrower goes into default. Furthermore, the rules governing foreclosures, and the length of time the process takes, vary by state.

Recent Market Trends

Home prices rose rapidly throughout some regions of the United States beginning in 2001. Housing has traditionally been seen as a safe investment that can offer an opportunity for high returns, and rapidly rising home prices reinforced this view. During this housing "boom," many people decided to buy homes or take out second mortgages in order to access their increasing home equity. Furthermore, rising home prices and low interest rates contributed to a sharp increase in people refinancing their mortgages; for example, between 2000 and 2003, the number of refinanced mortgage loans jumped from 2.5 million to over 15 million.[2] Around the same time, subprime lending, which generally refers to making mortgage loans to individuals with credit

---

[1] For a more detailed discussion of the foreclosure process and the factors that contribute to a lender's decision to pursue foreclosure, see CRS Report RL34232, *The Process, Data, and Costs of Mortgage Foreclosure*, by Darryl E. Getter et al.

[2] U.S. Department of Housing and Urban Development, Office of Policy Development and Research, *An Analysis of Mortgage Refinancing, 2001-2003*, November 2004, p.1, http://www.huduser.org/Publications/pdf/MortgageRefinance03.pdf

scores that are too low to qualify for prime rate mortgages, also began to increase, reaching a peak between 2004 and 2006. However, beginning in 2006 and 2007, home sales started to decline, home prices stopped rising and began to fall in many regions, and the rates of homeowners becoming delinquent on their mortgages or going into foreclosure began to increase.

The percentage of home loans in the foreclosure process in the U.S. has been rising rapidly since the middle of 2006. Although not all homes in the foreclosure process will end in a foreclosure completion, an increase in the number of loans in the foreclosure process is generally accompanied by an increase in the number of homes on which a foreclosure is completed. According to the Mortgage Bankers Association, an industry group, about 1% of all home loans were in the foreclosure process in the second quarter of 2006. By the third quarter of 2008, the rate had tripled to almost 3%.

The foreclosure rate for subprime loans has always been higher than the foreclosure rate for prime loans. For example, in the second quarter of 2006, just over 3.5% of subprime loans were in the foreclosure process compared to less than 0.5% of prime loans. However, both prime and subprime loans have seen similar increases in the foreclosure rate over the past several quarters. Like the foreclosure rate for all loans combined, the foreclosure rates for prime and subprime loans have both more than tripled, with the rate of subprime loans in the foreclosure process increasing to about 12.5% in Q3 2008 and the rate of prime loans in the foreclosure process increasing to just over 1.5% in the same period. According to the Congressional Budget Office (CBO), observers expect the high rate of foreclosures to continue in 2009 and beyond.[3]

---

[3] Statement of Douglas W. Elmendorf, Director, Congressional Budget Office, testimony before the U.S. Congress, Senate Committee on the Budget, *Federal Response to the Housing and Financial Crisis*, 111th Cong., 1st sess., January 28, 2009, p. 17, http://cbo.gov/ftpdocs/99xx/doc9971/01-28-FinancialMarkets_Testimony.pdf.

Notes: The Mortgage Bankers Association (MBA) is one of several organizations that reports delinquency and foreclosure data, but it does not represent all mortgages. MBA estimates that its data cover about 80% of the mortgage market

Impacts of Foreclosure

Losing a home to foreclosure can have a number of negative effects on a household. For many families, losing a home means losing the household's largest store of wealth. Furthermore, foreclosure can negatively impact a borrower's creditworthiness, making it more difficult for him or her to buy a home in the future. Finally, losing a home to foreclosure can also mean that a household loses many of the less tangible benefits of owning a home. Research has shown that these benefits include increased civic engagement that results from having a stake in the community, and better health, school, and behavioral outcomes for children.[4]

Some homeowners might have difficulty finding a place to live after losing their home to foreclosure. Many will become renters. However, some landlords may be unwilling to rent to families whose credit has been damaged by a foreclosure, limiting the options open to these families. There can also be spillover effects from foreclosure on current renters. Renters living in units facing foreclosure may be required to move, even if they are current on their rent payments. As more homeowners become renters and as more current renters are displaced when their landlords face foreclosure, pressure on local rental markets may increase, and more families may have difficulty finding affordable rental housing. Some observers have also raised the concern that a large increase in foreclosures could increase homelessness, either because families who lost their homes have trouble finding new places to live or because the increased demand for rental housing makes it more difficult for families to find adequate, affordable units.

If foreclosures are concentrated, they can also have negative impacts on communities. Many foreclosures in a single neighborhood may depress surrounding home values.[5] If foreclosed homes stand vacant for long periods of time, they can attract crime and blight, especially if they are not well maintained. Concentrated foreclosures also place pressure on local governments, which can lose property tax revenue and may have to step in to maintain vacant foreclosed properties.

The Policy Problem

There is a broad bipartisan consensus that the recent rapid rise in foreclosures is having negative consequences on households and communities. For example, Representative Spencer Bachus, Ranking Member of the House Committee on Financial Services, has said that "[i]t is in everyone's best interest as a general rule to prevent foreclosures. Foreclosures have a negative

---

[4] For example, see Donald R. Haurin, Toby L. Parcel, and R. Jean Haurin, *The Impact of Homeownership on Child Outcomes*, Joint Center for Housing Studies, Harvard University, Low-Income Homeownership Working Paper Series, October 2001, http://www.jchs.harvard.edu/publications/homeownership/liho01-14.pdf, and Denise DiPasquale and Edward L. Glaeser, *Incentives and Social Capital: Are Homeowners Better Citizens?*, National Bureau of Economic Research, NBER Working Paper 6363, Cambridge, MA, January 1998, http://www.nber.org/papers/w6363.pdf? new_window=1.

[5] For a review of the literature on the impact of foreclosures on nearby house prices, see Kai-yan Lee, *Foreclosure's Price-Depressing Spillover Effects on Local Properties: A Literature Review*, Federal Reserve Bank of Boston, Community Affairs Discussion Paper, No. 2008-01, September 2008, http://www.bos.frb.org/commdev/pcadp/2008/ pcadp0801.pdf.

impact not only on families but also on their neighbors, their property value, and on the community and local government."[6] Senator Chris Dodd, Chairman of the Senate Committee on Banking, Housing, and Urban Affairs, has described an "overwhelming tide of foreclosures ravaging our neighborhoods and forcing thousands of American families from their homes."[7]

There is less agreement among policymakers about how much the federal government should do to prevent foreclosures. Proponents of enacting government policies and using government resources to prevent foreclosures argue that, in addition to being a compassionate response to the plight of individual homeowners, such action may prevent further damage to home values and communities that can be caused by concentrated foreclosures. Supporters also suggest that preventing foreclosures may help stabilize the economy as a whole. Opponents of government foreclosure prevention programs argue that foreclosure prevention should be worked out between lenders and borrowers without government interference. Opponents also express concern that people who do not really need help, or who are not perceived to deserve help, will unfairly take advantage of government foreclosure prevention programs. They argue that taxpayers' money should not be used to help people who can still afford their loans but want to get more favorable terms, people who may be seeking to pass their losses on to the lender or the taxpayer, or people who knowingly took on mortgages that they could not afford.

Despite the concerns surrounding foreclosure prevention programs, and disagreement over the proper role of the government in preserving homeownership, Congress and the executive branch have both recently taken actions aimed at preventing foreclosures. Many private companies and state and local governments have also undertaken their own foreclosure prevention efforts. This report describes why so many households are currently at risk of foreclosure, outlines recent government and private initiatives to help homeowners remain in their homes, and discusses some of the challenges inherent in designing successful foreclosure prevention plans.

Why Might a Household Find Itself Facing Foreclosure?

There are many reasons that a household might fall behind on its mortgage payments. Some borrowers may have simply taken out loans on homes that they could not afford. However, many homeowners who believed they were acting responsibly when they took out a mortgage nonetheless find themselves facing foreclosure. The reasons households might have difficulty making their mortgage payments include changes in personal circumstances, which can be exacerbated by macroeconomic conditions, and features of the mortgages themselves.

Changes in Household Circumstances

Changes in a household's circumstances can affect its ability to pay its mortgage. For example, a number of events can leave a household with a lower income than it anticipated when it bought its home. Such changes in circumstances can include a lost job, an illness, or a change in family

---

[6] Representative Spencer Bachus, "Remarks of Ranking Member Spencer Bachus During Full Committee Hearing on Loan Modifications," press release, November 12, 2008, http://bachus.house.gov/HoR/AL06/Press+Room/Press+Releases/2008/111208Remarks+of+Ranking+Member+Spencer+Bachus+During+Full+Committee+Hearing+on+Loan+Modifications.htm.

[7] Senator Chris Dodd, "Dodd Statement on Government Loan Modification Program," statement, November 11, 2008, http://dodd.senate.gov/?q=node/4620.

structure due to divorce or death. Families that expected to maintain a certain level of income may struggle to make payments if a household member loses a job or faces a cut in pay, or if a two-earner household becomes a single-earner household. Unexpected medical bills or other unforeseen expenses can also make it difficult for a family to stay current on its mortgage.

Furthermore, sometimes a change in circumstances means that a home no longer meets a family's needs, and the household needs to sell the home. These changes can include having to relocate for a job or needing a bigger house to accommodate a new child or an aging parent. Traditionally, households that needed to move could usually sell their existing homes. However, the recent decline in home prices in many communities nationwide has left some homeowners "underwater," meaning that borrowers owe more on their homes than the house is worth. This limits homeowners' ability to sell their homes if they have to move; many of these families are effectively trapped in their current home and mortgage because they cannot afford to sell their home at a loss.

The risks presented by changing personal circumstances have always existed for anyone who took out a loan, but deteriorating macroeconomic conditions, such as falling home prices and increasing unemployment, have made families especially vulnerable to losing their homes for such reasons. The fall in home values that has left some homeowners owing more than the value of their homes not only traps those people in their current homes; it also makes it difficult for homeowners to sell their homes in order to avoid a foreclosure, and it increases the incentive for homeowners to walk away from their homes if they can no longer afford their mortgage payments. Along with the fall in home values, another recent macroeconomic trend has been increasing unemployment. More households experiencing job loss and the resultant income loss has made it difficult for many families to keep up with their monthly mortgage payments.

Mortgage Features

Borrowers might also find themselves having difficulty staying current on their loan payments due in part to features of their mortgages. In the last several years, there has been an increase in the use of alternative mortgage products whose terms differ significantly from the traditional 30-year, fixed interest rate mortgage model.[8] While borrowers with traditional mortgages are not immune to delinquency and foreclosure, many of these alternative mortgage features seem to have increased the risk that a homeowner will have trouble staying current on his or her mortgage. Many of these loans were structured to have low monthly payments in the early stages and then adjust to higher monthly payments depending on prevailing market interest rates and/or the length of time the borrower held the mortgage. Furthermore, many of these mortgage features made it more difficult for homeowners to quickly build equity in their homes. Some examples of the features of these alternative mortgage products are listed below.

Adjustable-Rate Mortgages

With an adjustable-rate mortgage (ARM), a borrower's interest rate can change at predetermined intervals, often based on changes in an index. The new interest rate can be higher or lower than

---

[8] For a fuller discussion of these types of mortgage products and their effects, see CRS Report RL33775, *Alternative Mortgages: Causes and Policy Implications of Troubled Mortgage Resets in the Subprime and Alt-A Markets*, by Edward V. Murphy.

the initial interest rate, and monthly payments can also be higher or lower based on both the new interest rate and any interest rate or payment caps.[9] Some ARMs also include an initial low interest rate known as a teaser rate. After the initial low-interest period ends and the new interest rate kicks in, the monthly payments that the borrower must make may increase, possibly by a significant amount.

Adjustable-rate mortgages make economic sense for some borrowers, especially if interest rates are expected to go down in the future. ARMs can help people own a home sooner than they may have been able to otherwise, or make sense for borrowers who cannot afford a high loan payment in the present but expect a significant increase in income in the future that would allow them to afford higher monthly payments. Furthermore, the interest rate on ARMs tends to follow short-term interest rates in the economy; if the gap between short-term and long-term rates gets very wide, it might make sense for borrowers to choose an ARM even if they expect interest rates to rise in the future. Finally, in markets with rising property values, borrowers with ARMs may be able to refinance their mortgages to avoid higher interest rates or large increases in monthly payments. However, if home prices fall, refinancing and selling the home to pay off the debt may not be feasible, and homeowners can find themselves stuck with higher mortgage payments.

Zero-Downpayment or Low-Downpayment Loans

As the name suggests, zero-downpayment and low-downpayment loans require either no downpayment or a significantly lower downpayment than has traditionally been required. These types of loans make it easier for homebuyers who do not have a lot of cash up-front to purchase a home. This type of loan may be especially useful in areas where home prices are rising more rapidly than income, because it allows borrowers without enough cash for a large downpayment to enter markets they could not otherwise afford. However, a low- or no-downpayment loan also means that families have little or no equity in their homes in the early phases of the mortgage, making it difficult to sell or refinance the home in response to a change in circumstances if home prices decline. Such loans may also mean that a homeowner takes out a larger mortgage than he or she would otherwise.

Interest-Only Loans and Negative Amortization Loans

With an interest-only loan, borrowers pay only the interest on a mortgage—but no part of the principal—for a set period of time. This option increases the homeowner's monthly payments in the future, after the interest-only period ends and the principal amortizes. These types of loans limit a household's ability to build equity in its home, making it difficult to sell or refinance the home in response to a change in circumstances if home prices are declining.

With a negative amortization loan, borrowers have the option to pay less than the full amount of the interest due for a set period of time. The loan "negatively amortizes" as the remaining interest is added to the outstanding loan balance. Like interest-only loans, this option increases future monthly mortgage payments when the principal and the balance of the interest amortizes. These

---

[9] Even if the interest rate remains the same or decreases, it is possible for monthly payments to increase if prior payments were subject to an interest rate cap or a payment cap. This is because unpaid interest that would have accrued if not for the cap can be added to the principal loan amount, resulting in negative amortization. For more information on the many variations of adjustable rate mortgages, see The Federal Reserve Board, *Consumer Handbook on Adjustable Rate Mortgages*, http://www.federalreserve.gov/pubs/arms/arms_english.htm#drop.

types of loans can be useful in markets where property values are rising rapidly, because borrowers can enter the market and then use the equity gained from rising home prices to refinance into loans with better terms before payments increase. They can also make sense for borrowers who currently have low incomes but expect a significant increase in income in the future. However, when home prices stagnate or fall, interest-only loans and negative amortization loans can leave borrowers with negative equity, making it difficult to refinance or sell the home to pay the mortgage debt.

Alt-A Loans

Alt-A loans are mortgages that are similar to prime loans, but for one or more reasons do not qualify for prime interest rates. One example of an Alt-A loan is a low-documentation or no-documentation loan. These are loans to borrowers with good credit scores but little or no income or asset documentation. Although no-documentation loans allow for more fraudulent activity on the part of both borrowers and lenders, they may be useful for borrowers with income that is difficult to document, such as those who are self-employed or work on commission. Other examples of Alt-A loans are loans with high loan-to-value ratios or loans to borrowers with credit scores that are too low for a prime loan but high enough to avoid a subprime loan. In all of these cases, the borrower is charged a higher interest rate than he or she would be charged with a prime loan.

Many of these loan features may have played a role in the recent increase in foreclosure rates. Some homeowners were current on their mortgages before their monthly payments increased due to interest rate resets or the end of option periods. Some built up little equity in their homes because they were not paying down the principal balance of their loan or because they had not made a downpayment. Stagnant or falling home prices in many regions also hampered borrowers' ability to build equity in their homes. Borrowers without sufficient equity find it difficult to take advantage of options such as refinancing into a more traditional mortgage if monthly payments become too high or selling the home if their personal circumstances change.

Types of Loan Workouts

When a household falls behind on its mortgage, there are options that lenders or servicers[10] may be able to employ as an alternative to beginning foreclosure proceedings. Some of these options, such as a short sale and a deed-in-lieu of foreclosure,[11] allow homeowners to avoid having a foreclosure on their record but still result in a household losing its home. This section describes

---

[10] Mortgage lenders are the organizations that make mortgage loans to individuals. Often, the mortgage is managed by a separate company known as a servicer; servicers usually have the most contact with the borrower, and are responsible for actions such as collecting mortgage payments, initiating foreclosures, and communicating with troubled borrowers. Finally, many mortgages are repackaged into mortgage-backed securities (MBS) that are sold to institutional investors. Servicers are usually subject to contracts with mortgage lenders and MBS investors that may limit their ability to undertake loan workouts or modifications; the scope of such contracts and the obligations that servicers must meet vary widely.

[11] In a short sale, a household sells its home for less than the amount it owes on its mortgage, and the lender generally accepts the proceeds from the sale as payment in full on the mortgage even though it is taking a loss. A deed-in-lieu of foreclosure refers to the practice of a borrower turning the deed to the house over to the lender, which accepts the deed as payment of the mortgage debt.

---

methods of avoiding foreclosure that allow homeowners to keep their homes; these options generally take the form of repayment plans or loan modifications.

Repayment Plans

A repayment plan allows a delinquent borrower to become up-to-date on his or her loan by paying back the payments he or she has missed, along with any accrued late fees. This is different from a loan modification, which changes one or more of the terms of the loan (such as the interest rate). Under a repayment plan, the missed payments and late fees may be paid back after the rest of the loan is paid off, or they may be added to the existing monthly payments. The first option increases the time that it will take for a borrower to pay back the loan, but his or her monthly payments will remain the same. The second option may result in an increase in monthly payments. Repayment plans may be a good option for homeowners who experienced a temporary loss of income but are now financially stable. However, since they do not generally make payments more affordable, repayment plans are unlikely to help homeowners with unaffordable loans avoid foreclosure in the long term.

Principal Forbearance

Principal forbearance means that a lender or servicer removes part of the principal from the portion of the loan balance that is subject to interest, thereby lowering borrowers' monthly payments by reducing the amount of interest owed. The portion of the principal that is subject to forbearance still needs to be repaid by the borrower in full, usually after the interest-bearing part of the loan is paid off or when the home is sold. Because principal forbearance does not actually change any of the loan terms, it resembles a repayment plan more than a loan modification.

Principal Write-Downs/Principal Forgiveness

A principal write-down is a type of mortgage modification that lowers borrowers' monthly payments by forgiving a portion of the loan's principal balance. The forgiven portion of the principal never needs to be repaid. Because the borrower now owes less, his or her monthly payment will be smaller. This option is costly for lenders but can help borrowers achieve affordable monthly payments, as well as increase the stake borrowers have in their homes and therefore increase their desire to stay current on the mortgage and avoid foreclosure.[12]

Interest Rate Reductions

Another form of loan modification is when the lender voluntarily lowers the interest rate on a mortgage. This is different from a refinance, in which a borrower takes out a new mortgage with a lower interest rate and uses the proceeds from the new loan to pay off the old loan. Unlike refinancing, a borrower does not have to pay closing costs or qualify for a new loan to get an interest rate reduction, which makes interest rate reductions a good option for borrowers who owe

---

[12] Historically, one impediment to principal forgiveness has been that borrowers were required to claim the forgiven amount as income, and therefore had to pay taxes on that income. Congress recently passed legislation that excludes mortgage debt forgiven before January 1, 2013 from taxable income. For more information about the tax treatment of principal forgiveness, see CRS Report RL34212, *Analysis of the Tax Exclusion for Canceled Mortgage Debt Income*, by Mark P. Keightley and Erika Lunder.

more on their mortgages than their homes are worth. With an interest rate reduction, the interest rate can be reduced permanently, or it can be reduced for a period of time before increasing again to a certain fixed point. Lenders can also freeze interest rates at their current level in order to avoid impending costly interest rate resets on adjustable rate mortgages. Interest rate modifications are relatively costly to the lender, but they can be effective at reducing monthly payments to an affordable level.

Extended Loan Term/Extended Amortization

Another option for lowering monthly mortgage payments is extending the amount of time over which the loan is paid back. While extending the loan term increases the total cost of the mortgage for the borrower because more interest will accrue, it allows monthly payments to be smaller because they are paid over a longer period of time. Most mortgages in the U.S. have an initial loan term of 25 or 30 years; extending the loan term from 30 to 40 years, for example, could result in a lower monthly mortgage payment for the borrower.

Recent Foreclosure Prevention Initiatives

Government Initiatives

To date, federal, state, and local governments have created a number of programs to attempt to stem the rise in foreclosures and help more homeowners remain in their homes. This section describes recent federal programs and briefly outlines some state and local foreclosure prevention efforts.

FHASecure

On August 31, 2007, the Federal Housing Administration (FHA) announced *FHASecure*, a temporary program allowing delinquent borrowers with non-FHA adjustable-rate mortgages (ARMs) to refinance into FHA-insured fixed-rate mortgages.[13] The new mortgage helps borrowers by offering better loan terms that either reduce a borrower's monthly payments or help a borrower avoid steep payment increases under his or her old loan. *FHASecure* expired on December 31, 2008.

To qualify for *FHASecure*, borrowers originally had to meet the following eligibility criteria:

- The borrower had a non-FHA ARM that had reset.

- The borrower became delinquent on his or her loan due to the reset, and had sufficient income to make monthly payments on the new FHA-insured loan.

- The borrower was current on his or her mortgage prior to the reset. (Some borrowers with a minimum amount of equity in their homes could still be eligible for the program even if they had missed payments prior to the reset.)

---

[13] FHA already offered refinancing options for homeowners who were current on their existing fixed- or adjustable-rate mortgages and continued to do so after the adoption of *FHASecure*.

- The new loan met standard FHA underwriting criteria and was subject to other standard FHA requirements (including maximum loan-to-value ratios, mortgage limits, and up-front and annual mortgage insurance premiums).

In July 2008, FHA expanded its eligibility criteria for the program, and borrowers had to meet the following revised eligibility requirements:

- The borrower became delinquent on his or her non-FHA ARM because of an interest rate reset or another extenuating circumstance, and had sufficient income to make monthly payments on the new FHA-insured loan.

- The borrower had no more than two payments that were thirty days late, or one payment that was sixty days late, in the twelve months preceding the interest rate reset or other extenuating circumstance.

- If the loan-to-value ratio on the FHA-insured mortgage was no higher than 90%, the borrower may have had no more than three payments that were thirty days late, or one payment that was ninety days late, prior to the interest rate reset or other extenuating circumstance.

- Borrowers with interest-only ARMs or option ARMs must have been delinquent due to an interest rate reset only (and not other extenuating circumstances), and must have been current on their mortgages prior to the reset; the revised eligibility criteria do not apply to these borrowers.

- The new loan met standard FHA underwriting criteria and was subject to other standard FHA requirements (including maximum loan-to-value ratios, mortgage limits, and up-front and annual mortgage insurance premiums).

FHASecure expired on December 31, 2008. In the months before its expiration, some housing policy advocates called for the program to be extended; however, HUD officials contended that continuing the program would be prohibitively expensive, possibly endangering FHA's single-family mortgage insurance program. HUD also points to the Hope for Homeowners program, described below, as filling the role that *FHASecure* did in helping households avoid foreclosure.[14] Supporters of extending *FHASecure* argue that the statutory requirements of Hope for Homeowners may offer less flexibility in the face of changing circumstances than *FHASecure*, which could have been more easily amended by HUD.

When *FHASecure* expired at the end of 2008, about 4,000 loans had been refinanced through the program.[15] Critics of the program point to the relatively stringent criteria that borrowers had to meet to qualify for the program as a possible reason that more people did not take advantage of it.

---

[14] HUD Mortgagee Letter 08-41, "Termination of *FHASecure*," December 19, 2008, available at http://www.hud.gov/offices/adm/hudclips/letters/mortgagee/2008ml.cfm.

[15] Congressional Budget Office, "The Budget and Economic Outlook: Fiscal Years 2009 to 2019," January 2009, available at http://www.cbo.gov/ftpdocs/99xx/doc9957/01-07-Outlook.pdf.

IndyMac Loan Modifications

On July 11, 2008, the Office of Thrift Supervision in the Department of the Treasury closed IndyMac Federal Savings Bank, based in Pasadena, California, and placed it under the conservatorship of the Federal Deposit Insurance Corporation (FDIC). In August 2008, the FDIC put into place a loan modification program for holders of mortgages either owned or serviced by IndyMac that were seriously delinquent or in danger of default, or on which the borrower was having trouble making payments because of interest rate resets or a change in financial circumstances.

The IndyMac program offers systematic loan modifications to qualified borrowers in financial trouble. The systematic approach means that all loan modifications follow the same basic formula to identify qualified borrowers and reduce their monthly payments in a uniform way. Such an approach is meant to allow more modifications to happen more quickly than if each loan was modified on a case-by-case basis.

In order to be eligible for a loan modification, the mortgage must be for the borrower's primary residence and the borrower must provide current income information that documents financial hardship. Furthermore, the expected future cost of the loan modification to the FDIC and the mortgage investors must be less than the expected future cost of foreclosure. This is sometimes referred to as the "net present value test," and it helps determine whether a loan modification makes financial sense for the lender as well as the borrower.

If a borrower meets the above conditions, the loan is modified so that he or she has a mortgage debt-to-income ratio (DTI) of 38%, meaning that the borrower's monthly mortgage payments (including principal, interest, taxes, and insurance) cannot exceed 38% of his or her monthly income. The goal is to lower a borrower's monthly payments to a level that is sustainable based on the borrower's current income. The 38% DTI can be achieved by lowering the interest rate, extending the period of the loan, forbearing a portion of the principal, or a combination of the three. The interest rate is set at the Freddie Mac survey rate for conforming mortgages, but if necessary it can be lowered for a period of up to five years in order to reach the 38% DTI; after the five-year period, the interest rate rises by no more than 1% each year until it reaches the Freddie Mac survey rate.

As of mid-December 2008, 7,500 loan modifications had been completed out of an estimated 40,000 eligible mortgages, and FDIC Chairman Sheila Bair expected "thousands" more to be modified in subsequent months.[16] On January 2, 2009, the FDIC announced an agreement to sell IndyMac to a group of investors. The new owners are required to continue the loan modification program after the sale.[17]

---

[16] Remarks by FDIC Chairman Sheila Bair to the New America Foundation conference "Did Low-Income Home Ownership Go Too Far?": Washington, D.C., December 17, 2008. A transcript of these remarks is available at http://www.fdic.gov/news/news/speeches/archives/2008/chairman/spdec1708.html

[17] Federal Deposit Insurance Corporation, "FDIC Board Approves Letter of Intent to Sell IndyMac Federal," press release, January 2, 2009, http://www.fdic.gov/news/news/press/2009/pr09001.html

Hope for Homeowners

Congress created the Hope for Homeowners program in the Housing and Economic Recovery Act of 2008 (P.L. 110-289), which was signed into law on July 30, 2008. The program, which is voluntary on the part of both borrowers and lenders, offers certain borrowers the ability to refinance into new mortgages insured by FHA if their lenders agree to certain loan modifications.

The Hope for Homeowners program began on October 1, 2008, and will remain in place until September 30, 2011. In order to be eligible for the program, borrowers must meet the following requirements:

- The borrower must have a mortgage that originated on or before January 1, 2008.

- The borrower's mortgage payments must have been more than 31% of their gross monthly income as of March 1, 2008.

- The borrower must not own another home.

- The borrower must not have intentionally defaulted on his or her mortgage, and he or she must not have been convicted of fraud during the last ten years under either federal or state law.

- The borrower must not have provided false information to obtain the original mortgage.

Under the original terms of the program, the lender agreed to write the mortgage down to 90% of the home's currently appraised value. The home therefore must be reappraised by an FHA-approved home appraiser in order to determine its current value, and the lender absorbs whatever loss results from this write-down. The new mortgage is a 30-year fixed-rate mortgage with no prepayment penalties, and may not exceed $550,440. Any second lien-holders were required to release their lien in exchange for a share of any future profit when the home is eventually sold. The homeowner pays an upfront mortgage insurance premium of 3%, and an annual mortgage insurance premium of 1.5%. When the homeowner sells or refinances the home, he or she must share between 50% and 100% of the proceeds with HUD depending on the length of time that passes between the time the borrower enters the program and when he or she sells the home. After one year, 100% of the equity in the home and any home value appreciation is shared with FHA, while after five years, only 50% is shared with FHA.

On November 19, 2008, HUD announced three changes to Hope for Homeowners in order to simplify the program and encourage participation.[18] These changes did the following: (1) increased the maximum loan-to-value ratio of the new loan to 96.5% of the home's currently appraised value, instead of the original 90%, in order to minimize losses to lenders; (2) allowed lenders to increase the term of the mortgage from 30 to 40 years in order to lower borrowers' monthly payments; and (3) offered an immediate payment to second lien-holders, instead of a share in future profits, in return for their agreement to relinquish the lien.

---

[18] The authority to make these changes to Hope for Homeowners was granted in P.L. 110-343, the Emergency Economic Stabilization Act of 2008. The decision to make the changes was ultimately made by the Board of Hope for Homeowners, which includes the Secretary of HUD and the Secretary of the Treasury, among others.

The CBO originally estimated that up to 400,000 homeowners could be helped to avoid foreclosure over the life of the program.[19] As of February 3, 2009, the program had received 451 applications and 25 new mortgages had closed.[20] Some have suggested that more borrowers and lenders have not used Hope for Homeowners because the program requires so many players to take losses: lenders must write down part of the principal, and borrowers must share future equity in their homes and any home price appreciation. Others have suggested that borrowers and lenders have been hesitant to use the program as long as interest in developing other foreclosure prevention plans continues, in case a new plan is enacted that offers more favorable terms.

Lawmakers have recently proposed additional legislative changes to the Hope for Homeowners program. H.R. 1106, the Helping Families Save Their Homes Act of 2009, would reduce the upfront and annual mortgage insurance premiums to no more than 2% and 1%, respectively, and would allow servicers to receive incentive payments of $1,000 for each loan successfully modified. The bill would also place the Hope for Homeowners program under the control of the Secretary of Housing and Urban Development, and would limit eligibility for the program to homeowners whose net worth does not exceed a certain threshold.

Fannie Mae and Freddie Mac

On November 11, 2008, James Lockhart, the director of the Federal Housing Finance Agency (FHFA), which oversees Fannie Mae and Freddie Mac,[21] announced a new Streamlined Modification Program (SMP) that Fannie, Freddie, and certain private mortgage lenders and servicers planned to undertake.[22] Fannie Mae and Freddie Mac had helped troubled borrowers through individualized loan modifications for some time, but the SMP represents an attempt to formalize the process and set an industry standard. The SMP took effect on December 15, 2008. On November 20, 2008, Fannie Mae and Freddie Mac also announced that they would suspend foreclosure sales and evictions between November 26, 2008 and January 9, 2009, in order to have time to reach out to borrowers who might be eligible for loan modifications under the SMP. Fannie and Freddie later extended the moratorium through the end of February 2009.

In order for borrowers whose mortgages are owned by Fannie Mae or Freddie Mac to be eligible for the SMP, they must meet the following criteria:

---

[19] Congressional Budget Office, Cost Estimate, *Federal Housing Finance Regulatory Reform Act of 2008*, June 9, 2008, p. 8, http://www.cbo.gov/ftpdocs/93xx/doc9366/Senate_Housing.pdf.

[20] Written statement of Meg Burns, Director, Office of Single Family Program Development, U.S. Department of Housing and Urban Development, testimony before the U.S. Congress, House Committee on Financial Services, *Promoting Bank Liquidity and Lending through Deposit Insurance, Hope for Homeowners, and other Enhancements*, 111th Cong., 1st sess., February 3, 2009, http://www.house.gov/apps/list/hearing/financialsvcs_dem/burns020309.pdf.

[21] Fannie Mae and Freddie Mac are government-sponsored enterprises (GSEs) that were chartered by Congress to provide liquidity to the mortgage market. Rather than make loans directly, the GSEs buy loans made in the private market and either hold them in their own portfolios or securitize and sell them to investors. The GSEs were put under the conservatorship of FHFA on September 7, 2008. For more information on the GSEs in general, see CRS Report RL33756, *Fannie Mae and Freddie Mac: A Legal and Policy Overview*, by N. Eric Weiss and Michael V. Seitzinger, and for more information on the conservatorship, see CRS Report RS22950, *Fannie Mae and Freddie Mac in Conservatorship*, by Mark Jickling.

[22] The private mortgage lenders and servicers who are participating in the Streamlined Modification Program are primarily members of the HOPE NOW Alliance, a voluntary alliance of industry members that formed to help homeowners avoid foreclosure. The HOPE NOW Alliance, and its involvement with the SMP, is described in detail in this report.

- The mortgage must have originated on or before January 1, 2008.
- The mortgage must have a loan-to-value ratio of at least 90%.
- The home must be a single-family residence occupied by the borrower, and it must be the borrower's primary residence.
- The borrower must have missed at least three mortgage payments.
- The borrower must not have filed for bankruptcy.

Mortgages that are insured or guaranteed by the federal government, such as those guaranteed FHA, the Veterans' Administration, or the Rural Housing Service, are not eligible for the SMP.

The SMP shares many features of the FDIC's plan to modify troubled mortgages held by IndyMac. Borrowers who qualify for the program must provide income information that is current within the last 90 days to the mortgage servicer. Based on this updated income information, borrowers' monthly mortgage payments will be lowered so that the household's mortgage debt-to-income ratio is 38% (this does not include second lien payments). After borrowers successfully complete a three-month trial period (by making all of the payments at the proposed modified payment amount), the loan modification automatically takes effect.

In order to reach the 38% mortgage debt-to-income ratio (DTI), servicers must follow a specific formula. First, the servicer capitalizes late payments and accrued interest (late fees and penalties must be waived). If this results in a DTI of 38% or less, the modification is complete. If the DTI is higher than 38%, the servicer can extend the term of the loan to up to forty years from the effective date of the modification. If the DTI is still above 38%, the interest rate can be adjusted to the current market rate or lower, but no less than 3%. Finally, if the DTI is still above 38% after the first three steps have been taken, servicers can offer principal forbearance. The amount of the principal forbearance will not accrue interest and is non-amortizing, but it will result in a balloon payment when the loan is paid off or the home is sold.

Negative amortization is not allowed under the SMP, nor are principal forgiveness or principal write-downs. In order to encourage participation in the SMP, Fannie Mae and Freddie Mac will pay servicers $800 for each loan modification completed through the program. If the SMP does not produce an affordable payment for the borrower, servicers will work with borrowers in a customized fashion to try to modify the loan in a way that the homeowner can afford.

Federal Reserve

On January 27, 2009, the Federal Reserve announced a plan to prevent foreclosures on mortgages it owns or controls, such as those it received as collateral for lending to troubled banks. According to initial reports, the plan will use interest rate reductions, extensions of the loan term, and principal forbearance and forgiveness to help struggling borrowers avoid foreclosure.

The Homeowner Affordability and Stability Plan

On February 18, 2009, President Obama announced the Homeowner Affordability and Stability Plan (HASP), aimed at helping homeowners who are having difficulty making their mortgage payments avoid foreclosure.[23] This plan is part of the Administration's broader economic recovery strategy, along with the Financial Stability Plan (an administrative initiative aimed at shoring up the financial system) and the American Recovery and Reinvestment Act of 2009 (enacted legislation (P.L. 111-5) aimed at stimulating the economy).[24] HASP includes three main parts.

The first part of HASP allows homeowners with mortgages owned or guaranteed by Fannie Mae or Freddie Mac who owe between 80% and 105% of the value of their homes to refinance into loans with more favorable terms. Currently, borrowers who owe more than 80% of the value of their homes have difficulty refinancing. This part of the plan is expected to help between 4 and 5 million homeowners.

The second part of the plan encourages servicers to provide mortgage modifications for troubled borrowers in order to reduce the borrowers' monthly mortgage payments to no more than 31% of their monthly income. The government will provide some assistance in lowering borrowers' monthly payments, and will also provide incentive payments to servicers who modify loans. The loan modification piece of the plan is expected to cost $75 billion and to help 3 to 4 million homeowners.

The third piece of HASP provides additional financial support for Fannie Mae and Freddie Mac in an effort to maintain low mortgage interest rates.

Foreclosure Counseling Funding to NeighborWorks America

Another federal effort to slow the rising number of foreclosures has been to appropriate funding for housing counseling.[25] This funding is primarily channeled through NeighborWorks America, a non-profit created by Congress in 1978 that has a national network of community partners. NeighborWorks traditionally provides housing counseling to homebuyers and homeowners, and since 2004 has also provided foreclosure intervention counseling. NeighborWorks also trains other non-profit housing counseling organizations in foreclosure counseling.

The Housing and Economic Recovery Act of 2008 (P.L. 110-289), appropriated $150 million for NeighborWorks to distribute to qualified organizations for foreclosure prevention counseling activities. P.L. 110-289 also appropriated an additional $30 million for NeighborWorks to distribute to counseling organizations to provide legal help to homeowners facing delinquency or foreclosure, giving priority to communities with the highest foreclosure rates and organizations that could use the money quickly. These amounts are in addition to $180 million appropriated to NeighborWorks in the Consolidated Appropriations Act 2008 (P.L. 110-161) to distribute for

---

[23] More information on the Housing Affordability and Stability Plan can be found on the Department of Housing and Urban Development's website at http://www.hud.gov/initiatives/homeowner/index.cfm.

[24] For more information on the Financial Stability Plan, see http://www.financialstability.gov/docs/fact-sheet.pdf. For more information on the American Recovery and Reinvestment Act of 2009, see CRS Report R40104, *Economic Stimulus: Issues and Policies*, by Jane G. Gravelle, Thomas L. Hungerford, and Marc Labonte.

[25] For each of the past several years, Congress has appropriated funding for various types of housing counseling, including pre-purchase counseling and post-purchase counseling, to be distributed to housing counseling agencies that have been certified by the Department of Housing and Urban Development.

foreclosure prevention activities, with a focus on areas with high foreclosure rates and on the subprime market.

State and Local Initiatives

In addition to federal efforts to prevent foreclosures, a number of state and local governments have implemented their own programs aimed at helping homeowners stay in their homes. Some of these efforts include supporting voluntary or mandatory pre-foreclosure counseling initiatives, imposing foreclosure moratoriums, providing short-term loans to help homeowners at risk of foreclosure, enacting stronger reporting requirements on lenders' loan modification efforts, and initiating legal actions. Many states and localities have also implemented educational efforts to reach out to troubled homeowners.

According to the Pew Charitable Trusts Center on the States, as of April 2008, twenty states have laws or regulations involving foreclosure mitigation, 24 states have statewide counseling efforts, 13 states have a foreclosure intervention hotline, and 9 states have developed loan funds to help homeowners refinance into more affordable mortgages or to provide short-term loans to borrowers facing foreclosure. Furthermore, at least 14 states have created foreclosure prevention task forces to attempt to address the problem of rising foreclosure rates.[26]

Private Initiatives

While the government has initiated the mortgage modification programs described above, a number of private mortgage lenders and servicers have voluntarily attempted to implement their own foreclosure prevention initiatives. Many private lenders have engaged in ongoing individual loan modifications for some time, but have recently launched more targeted programs to help troubled borrowers. This section describes some of these programs in order to provide illustrative examples of private sector initiatives to prevent foreclosures; it is not intended to be a comprehensive list of private foreclosure prevention efforts.

HOPE NOW Alliance

The HOPE NOW Alliance is a voluntary alliance of mortgage servicers, lenders, investors, counseling agencies, and others that formed in October 2007. The alliance is a private sector initiative created with the encouragement of the federal government to engage in active outreach efforts to troubled borrowers. Member organizations identify borrowers who may have difficulty making loan payments before they became seriously delinquent on their mortgages, and work with such borrowers to work out loan modifications that can keep the borrowers in their homes. When the alliance was first announced, eleven mortgage servicers were involved; by November 2008, twenty-seven servicers had become member organizations.

HOPE NOW Alliance members have undertaken several initiatives to help troubled homeowners. One such initiative the alliance has supported is a hotline, operated by the Homeownership Preservation Foundation, that connects borrowers to HUD-approved housing counselors who can

---

[26] The Pew Charitable Trusts Center on the States, *Defaulting on the Dream: States Respond to America's Foreclosure Crisis*, April 2008,
http://www.pewcenteronthestates.org/uploadedFiles/PCS_DefaultingOnTheDream_Report_FINAL041508_01.pdf

help homeowners contact their servicers and work out a plan to avoid foreclosure. The hotline serves as a first point of contact for troubled borrowers, and both HUD and non-profit organizations such as NeighborWorks America advocate its use.[27]

HOPE NOW also encourages its lenders and servicers to coordinate their efforts to modify mortgages. On December 6, 2007, the HOPE NOW Alliance announced a streamlined plan that would allow servicers to freeze the interest rate on certain subprime ARMs for borrowers who were current on their mortgages but would not be able to afford higher payments after their rates reset. While the plan received assurances from the government that the modifications would not affect certain accounting or tax issues surrounding securitized loans, servicers who went forward with modifications could not be certain that investors would not mount legal challenges.[28] Most recently, HOPE NOW announced on November 11, 2008 that most of its servicers would participate in the SMP, with the idea that the plan will create a new industry-wide approach to mortgage modifications.

According to HOPE NOW's own reports, the alliance expected to prevent 2.2 million foreclosures and complete almost 950,000 loan modifications in 2008 through these efforts.[29] However, some of these prevented foreclosures are the result of solutions other than loan modifications. These other solutions could include repayment plans, under which it is possible that some borrowers could end up with higher, not lower, monthly payments, and which may not substantially reduce the risk that these homeowners will eventually end up in default or foreclosure. They could also involve short sales or deeds-in-lieu-of-foreclosure, in which the homeowner avoids having a foreclosure on his or her financial record but still loses the home.

Bank of America

On October 6, 2008, Bank of America announced a loan modification program for homeowners whose mortgages are serviced by Countrywide (Countrywide was acquired by Bank of America on July 1, 2008.)[30] The program became effective December 1, 2008, and targets borrowers who are seriously delinquent, or in danger of becoming seriously delinquent, on their mortgages due to loan features such as interest rate resets.

The Bank of America program aims to reduce borrowers' mortgage debt to no more than 34% of gross monthly income for the first year of the modification. Subsequent rises in the interest rate or other loan terms are structured in a way that minimizes payment shock to the borrower. Types of loan modifications can include using the Hope for Homeowners program, described above, to help homeowners refinance into FHA-insured mortgages; reducing the interest rate; and reducing

---

[27] The phone number for the HOPE NOW Alliance hotline is 888-995-HOPE (4673).

[28] For more information on the tax and accounting issues surrounding this plan, see CRS Report RL34372, *The HOPE NOW Alliance/American Securitization Forum (ASF) Plan to Freeze Certain Mortgage Interest Rates*, by David H. Carpenter and Edward V. Murphy.

[29] The HOPE NOW Alliance, "HOPE NOW Projects Big Increases in Foreclosure Prevention Successes in 2009," press release, Dec. 22, 2008, available online at
http://hopenow.com/upload/press_release/files/HOPE%20NOW%202008%20Year%20End%20Release.pdf

[30] Bank of America, "Bank of America Announces Nationwide Homeownership Retention Program for Countrywide Customers," press release, October 6, 2008,
http://newsroom.bankofamerica.com/index.php?s=press_releases&item=8272

the principal balance on option-ARMs. Eligibility for the program is limited to primary residences.

JP Morgan Chase

On October 31, 2008, JP Morgan Chase announced an expansion of its foreclosure prevention efforts.[31] This expansion includes reaching out to borrowers before they begin to miss payments, and conducting a systematic review of all of the mortgages held by Chase to ascertain which borrowers might be eligible for loan modifications. Chase will offer troubled borrowers a combination of reductions in their interest rate and principal forbearance, and will review each mortgage before it enters the foreclosure process to ensure that eligible borrowers were offered loan modifications. Chase specifically excludes negative amortization as a loan modification option. Chase also announced that it would not begin any foreclosures while the expanded program was being implemented.

In order to be eligible for a loan modification, borrowers must have a mortgage that is owned by Chase, Washington Mutual, or EMC. (EMC and Washington Mutual were acquired by JP Morgan Chase in March 2008 and September 2008, respectively.) If a borrower's mortgage is serviced, but not owned, by one of these companies, the investors must give permission for the loan to be modified. To be eligible, borrowers must occupy the home as their primary residence.

Citigroup

On November 11, 2008, Citigroup announced that it was streamlining its existing mortgage modification program in the mold of the IndyMac loan modification model.[32] Under the streamlined program, Citigroup uses a formula to arrive at a certain mortgage payment-to-income ratio, and then uses a combination of interest rate reductions, extensions of the loan term, or forgiveness of part of the principal in order to reach that ratio. Citigroup also announced the Citi Homeowner Assistance program, in which it pledged to reach out to borrowers who were not yet delinquent on their mortgages but who were in danger of falling behind on their loan payments. Through this program, Citigroup plans to concentrate its efforts on geographic areas that are especially economically hard-hit, such as those areas experiencing steep home price declines or rapid rises in unemployment. Finally, Citigroup has announced a foreclosure moratorium in order to give it more time to reach out to borrowers and complete loan modifications.

Currently, these programs are in effect for mortgage loans that Citigroup owns. Citi is working with investors to expand the program to includes mortgages that are serviced, but not owned, by Citigroup.

---

[31] JP Morgan Chase, "Chase Further Strengthens Robust Programs to Keep Families in Homes," press release, October 31, 2008, http://files.shareholder.com/downloads/ONE/514430481x0x245621/b879b4eb-40c0-43f8-8614-6f2113759d0c/344473.pdf.

[32] Citigroup, "Citi Announces New Preemptive Initiatives to Help Homeowners Remain in Their Homes," press release, November 11, 2008, http://www.citigroup.com/citi/press/2008/081111a.htm

---

Other Foreclosure Prevention Proposals

Some observers argue that the programs outlined above, which have already been implemented by various government and private organizations, have not been effective enough at stopping the rising foreclosure rate and keeping people in their homes. There have been calls for the government to do more to help homeowners. This section briefly outlines some existing proposals for further action to help prevent foreclosures.

Changing Bankruptcy Law

One method that has been suggested to help more homeowners remain in their homes is to amend bankruptcy law to allow a judge to order a mortgage loan modification as part of a bankruptcy proceeding. Bankruptcy judges currently have the authority to modify or reduce other types of outstanding debt obligations, including mortgages on second homes and vacation homes, but this authority does not extend to mortgages on primary residences. Opponents of such a change do not want judges to have such broad power to amend a contract after the fact. They argue that allowing these "cramdowns" would make lenders more hesitant to make mortgage loans in the future, since the threat of a loan being modified in this way could make mortgage lending more risky. Supporters of amending bankruptcy law say that, in addition to helping a borrower in bankruptcy avoid foreclosure through a court-mandated loan modification, such a change might also encourage lenders to work with borrowers to modify loans before the bankruptcy process begins in the first place. Provisions to amend bankruptcy law to allow judges to modify mortgages on primary residences are included in H.R. 1106, the Helping Families Save Their Homes Act of 2009. (For a description of the bankruptcy process and recent legislative proposals to amend bankruptcy law to allow judges to order mortgage modifications, see CRS Report RL34301, *The Primary Residence Exception: Legislative Proposals in the 111th Congress to Amend the Bankruptcy Code to Allow the Strip Down of Certain Home Mortgages*, by David H. Carpenter.)

Foreclosure Moratorium

Some advocates have called for placing a temporary moratorium on foreclosure completions. Proponents of this idea argue that placing a freeze on foreclosure completions would give homeowners and lenders more time to work out sustainable loan modifications that would allow the homeowner to remain in the home and turn troubled mortgages back into performing loans that benefit the lenders. Opponents of a foreclosure moratorium argue that the government should not interfere with the right of a lender to complete foreclosure proceedings against a borrower who has defaulted on his or her loan. They note that delaying foreclosure proceedings through a foreclosure moratorium could result in greater losses for the lender if the ultimate outcome is still a foreclosure and the home's price has fallen further in the interim.

Fannie Mae, Freddie Mac, and some private lenders have instituted temporary foreclosure moratoriums while they put foreclosure prevention programs in place. While a wider foreclosure moratorium had widely been considered a radical idea until recently, the severity of the increase in foreclosures and its impact on the economy has led some to give the idea serious consideration. (For an analysis of the economic principals behind a foreclosure moratorium, see CRS Report RL34653, *Economic Analysis of a Mortgage Foreclosure Moratorium*, by Edward V. Murphy. For an analysis of the legal issues involved, see CRS Report RL34369, *Constitutional Issues*

Relating to Proposals for Foreclosure Moratorium Legislation That Affects Existing Mortgages, by David H. Carpenter.)

Federal Deposit Insurance Corporation Plan

As described earlier, the FDIC implemented a loan modification program for troubled homeowners whose mortgages were owned by IndyMac after the agency took over the bank in July 2008. Sheila Bair, chairman of the FDIC, has been a vocal advocate of implementing a wider foreclosure prevention plan based on the IndyMac model. According to Chairman Bair, a plan in which the government guarantees modified loans could help 1.5 million homeowners remain in their homes at a cost of $24 billion.[33] The FDIC plan would be a streamlined, methodical loan modification program resembling the IndyMac program. However, it would be more widely available to most homeowners who are having difficulty staying current on their mortgages, and the government would provide guarantees on the modified mortgages. Like the IndyMac program, homeowners would only be eligible for a loan modification if the lender would receive a greater expected return through a loan modification than through foreclosure.

Use of TARP Funds

The Emergency Economic Stabilization Act of 2008 (EESA, P.L. 110-343) was signed into law on October 3, 2008, and created the Troubled Assets Relief Program (TARP). A stated purpose of EESA is "preserv[ing] homeownership."[34] Some policymakers have suggested using TARP funds to directly fund foreclosure prevention programs, or using the funding and authority granted by EESA to encourage their adoption by private entities.

Issues and Challenges Associated with Preventing Foreclosures

There are several challenges associated with designing successful programs to prevent foreclosures. Some of these challenges are practical and concern issues surrounding the implementation of loan modifications. Other challenges are more conceptual, and are related to questions of fairness and precedent. This section describes some of the most prominent considerations involved in programs to preserve homeownership.

Who Has The Authority to Modify Mortgages?

In recent years, the practice of lenders packaging mortgages into securities and selling them to investors has become more widespread. This practice is known as securitization, and the securities that include the mortgages are known as mortgage-backed securities (MBS). When mortgages are sold through securitization, several players become involved with any individual

---

[33] Remarks by FDIC Chairman Sheila Bair to the New America Foundation conference "Did Low-Income Home Ownership Go Too Far?": Washington, D.C., December 17, 2008. A transcript of these remarks is available at http://www.fdic.gov/news/news/speeches/archives/2008/chairman/spdec1708.html.

[34] P.L. 110-343, Division A, Section 2. This section will be codified at 12 U.S.C. § 5201.

mortgage loan, including the lender, the servicer, and the investors who hold shares in the MBS. The servicer is usually the organization that has the most contact with the borrower, including receiving monthly payments and initiating any foreclosure proceedings. However, servicers are usually subject to contracts with investors which limit the activities that the servicer can undertake and require it to safeguard the investors' profit. One major question facing foreclosure prevention programs, therefore, is who actually has the authority to make a loan modification. Contractual obligations may limit the amount of flexibility that servicers have to modify loans in ways that could arguably yield a lower return for investors. In some cases, loan modifications can result in less of a loss for investors than foreclosure; however, lenders and servicers may not want to risk having investors challenge their assessment that a modification is more cost-effective than a foreclosure. This problem can be especially salient in streamlined programs in which large numbers of loans are modified at once. With such streamlined programs, the cost-effectiveness of loan modifications depends on questions such as how many loans would have likely ended up in foreclosure without the modification, making it more difficult to say whether wholesale loan modifications are in the best interest of investors.

H.R. 1106, the Helping Families Save Their Homes Act of 2009, would provide a safe harbor for servicers who engage in modifications of certain mortgages. A servicer safe harbor may make servicers more willing to undertake voluntary loan modifications.

Volume of Delinquencies and Foreclosures

Another issue facing loan modification programs is the sheer number of delinquencies and foreclosure proceedings underway. Lenders and servicers have a limited number of employees to reach out to troubled borrowers and find solutions. Contacting borrowers—some of whom may avoid contact with their servicer out of embarrassment or fear—and working out large numbers of individual loan modifications can overwhelm the capacity of the lenders and servicers who are trying to help homeowners avoid foreclosure. Streamlined plans that use a formula to modify all loans that meet certain criteria may make it easier for lenders and servicers to help a greater number of borrowers in a shorter amount of time. However, streamlined plans are more likely to run into the contractual issues between servicers and investors described above.

Possibility of Re-Default

Another major challenge associated with loan modification programs is the possibility that a homeowner who receives a modification will nevertheless default on the loan again in the future. This possibility is especially problematic if the home's value is falling, because in that case delaying an eventual foreclosure reduces the value that the lender can recoup through a foreclosure sale. Data released by the Comptroller of the Currency and the Office of Thrift Supervision show that 37% of loans modified in the first quarter of 2008 were 30 or more days delinquent again three months after the modification, and 55% were 30 or more days delinquent six months after the modification. The same data show that a smaller percentage of modified loans were 60 or more days delinquent: 19% of loans were 60 or more days delinquent three months after the modification, and 37% were 60 or more days delinquent 60 or more days after the modification.[35] Opponents of aggressive loan modification programs point to these data as

---

[35] Office of the Comptroller of the Currency and Office of Thrift Supervision, "OCC and OTS Mortgage Metrics Report: Disclosure of National Bank and Federal Thrift Mortgage Loan Data, Third Quarter 2008," December 2008, (continued...)

evidence that loan modifications are not effective at preventing foreclosures. However, proponents of such programs argue that the definition of loan modification used in these data is overly broad, and that many of the modifications did not actually result in lower monthly payments for the borrower.[36] These supporters believe that loan modifications that focus on creating truly affordable payments for troubled borrowers will exhibit lower rates of re-default.

Fairness Issues

Opponents of some foreclosure prevention plans argue that it is not fair to help homeowners who have fallen behind on their mortgages while homeowners who have been scraping by to stay current receive no help. Others argue that borrowers who got in over their heads, particularly if they intentionally took out mortgages that they knew they could not afford, should face consequences. Supporters of loan modification plans point out that many borrowers go into foreclosure for reasons outside of their control, and that some troubled borrowers may have been victims of deceptive, unfair, or fraudulent lending practices. Furthermore, a case can be made that foreclosure prevention programs are necessary not only out of compassion for the homeowner, but because foreclosures can create problems for other homeowners in the neighborhood by dragging down property values or putting a strain on local governments.

To address these concerns about fairness, some loan modification programs reach out to borrowers who are struggling to make payments but are not yet delinquent on their mortgage. Most programs also specifically exclude individuals who provided false information in order to obtain a mortgage.

Incentives

Another challenge is that loan modification programs may provide an incentive for borrowers to intentionally miss payments or default on their mortgage in order to qualify for a loan modification that provides more favorable mortgage terms. While many of the programs described above, including Hope for Homeowners, specifically require that a borrower must not have intentionally missed payments on his or her mortgage in order to qualify for the program, it can be difficult to prove a person's intention. Programs that are designed to reach out to distressed borrowers before they miss any payments, as well as those who are already delinquent, may minimize the incentive for homeowners to intentionally fall behind on their mortgage in order to receive help.

Precedent

Some opponents of government efforts to provide or encourage loan modifications argue that changing the terms of a contract retroactively sets a troubling precedent for future mortgage loans. These opponents argue that if lenders believe that they could be forced to change the terms

---

(...continued)

pp. 18-19, available at http://www.occ.treas.gov/ftp/release/2008-150a.pdf.

[36] Remarks by FDIC Chairman Sheila Bair to the New America Foundation conference "Did Low-Income Home Ownership Go Too Far?": Washington, D.C., December 17, 2008. A transcript of these remarks is available at http://www.fdic.gov/news/news/speeches/archives/2008/chairman/spdec1708.html

---

of a mortgage in the future, they will be less likely to provide mortgage loans in the first place or will only do so at higher interest rates to counter the perceived increase in the risk of not being repaid in full. Most existing programs attempt to address this concern by limiting the program's scope. These programs apply only to mortgages that originated during a certain time frame, and end at a pre-determined date.

Appendix. Comparison of Recent Federal Foreclosure Prevention Initiatives

Table A-1. Features of Selected Programs

Program/Initiative	Basic Eligibility Requirements	Program Details	Status
FHASecure	Borrower had a non-FHA ARM Borrower was delinquent due to an interest rate reset or other extenuating circumstances Home was occupied as primary residence Borrower had sufficient income to pay new loan Borrower missed no more than a minimum number of payments prior to reset or onset of extenuating circumstances (or had sufficient equity in the home)	Borrower contacted lender to determine eligibility Borrower refinanced into new, fixed-rate, FHA-insured mortgage Borrower's new loan met standard FHA underwriting criteria Borrower met other standard FHA requirements, such as paying FHA insurance premiums	Announced August 31, 2007. Expired Dec. 31, 2008 Estimated to have served about 4,000 homeowners
FDIC IndyMac modificatons	Borrower has a loan owned or serviced by IndyMac Borrower is (1) seriously delinquent or in danger of default, or (2) having trouble making mortgage payments due to interest rate resets or changes in financial circumstances Home is occupied as primary residence Borrower provides current income information documenting financial hardship Loan modification meets "net present value test," meaning that the loan modification must be less costly for FDIC than foreclosure	FDIC contacts eligible borrowers, but also encourages troubled homeowners to contact FDIC or IndyMac to see if they qualify Mortgages are systematically modified to achieve monthly payments of no more than 38% of borrowers' monthly income Achieves 38% mortgage debt-to-income ratio by a combination of lowering the interest rate, extending the loan term, or forbearing part of the principal	Active; announced July 11, 2008 As of mid-December 2008, had served about 7,500 homeowners out of an estimated 40,000 who were eligible; more modifications were expected to take place

Program/Initiative	Basic Eligibility Requirements	Program Details	Status
HOPE for Homeowners	Borrower has a non-FHA mortgage and lender agrees to participate Borrower is at risk of default or foreclosure Home is occupied as primary residence Borrower has experienced financial hardship and has total monthly mortgage payments higher than 31% of gross monthly income Mortgage originated on or after January 1, 2008, and at least 6 payments have been made Borrower does not have a fraud conviction in the last 10 years, has not intentionally defaulted, and did not provide false information to obtain original mortgage	Borrower contacts lender to determine eligibility Borrower refinances into FHA-insured fixed rate mortgage for 96.5% of home's currently appraised value (mortgage may not exceed $550,440) Lender absorbs loss resulting from write-down in mortgage value Borrower shares equity in home with FHA when the home is sold Borrower pays up-front and annual mortgage insurance premiums Second lien-holders release their liens in exchange for an upfront payment	Active; began October 1, 2008, and slated to expire September 30, 2011 As of February 3, 2009, 451 applications had been received and 25 loans had closed out of about 400,000 homeowners that were originally estimated could be served
Fannie Mae and Freddie Mac Streamlined Modification Plan	Borrower has a loan owned by Fannie Mae or Freddie Mac Borrower has missed three or more monthly payments Home is occupied as primary residence Mortgage loan-to-value ratio is at least 90% Mortgage originated on or before January 1, 2008 Borrower is not in active bankruptcy	Borrower contacts lender to determine eligibility Mortgages are systematically modified to achieve 38% mortgage debt-to-income ratio Modification follows the following steps in order as necessary to achieve 38% DTI: (1) capitalize late payments and accrued interest; (2) extend loan term for up to four years from modification date; (3) adjust interest rate to no lower than 3%; (4) principal forbearance. Servicers receive payment for each modification completed	Active; began December 15, 2008 No information on completed loan modifications currently available

Source: Table created by CRS.

Notes: The Federal Reserve announced a foreclosure prevention program on January 27, 2009. Details on this program will be added as they become available.

Author Contact Information

Katie Jones
Analyst in Housing Policy
kmjones@crs.loc.gov, 7-4162